CW00471233

EVERY SWING
SHOULD HAVE A TREE
AND OTHER POEMS

❧ BY ❧

BETTY FARBER

Houts & Home Publications LLC
Maryville, Missouri

*This book is dedicated to my mother and my husband with love
and admiration.*
– Betty Farber

Thank you to my daughters, Nancy Browning, for her valuable
editing, and Amy Houts, for her professional publishing, of this
book of poems.

Visit Nancy's website: https://www.expectgreatediting.com
Visit Amy's website: https://www.houtsandhome.com

Cover Design: Megg Houts
Interior design: Megg Houts

© 2024 by Betty Farber
All rights reserved. No part of this publication may be repro-
duced, stored in retrieval systems, or transmitted in any form or
by any means, electronic, photocopying, mechanical, recording,
or otherwise, without prior written permission of Betty Farber
or Houts & Home Publications LLC.

Printed in the United States of America
ISBN: 979-8-218-35816-7

For inquiries contact:
Amy Houts, President, Houts & Home Publications LLC
Maryville, Missouri 64468
Cell phone: 660.582.1426
Email: houtsandhome@gmail.com
Website: https://www.houtsandhome.com

Library of Congress Control Number: 2024905853

TABLE OF CONTENTS

A BEAUTIFUL DAY ON FIRST AVENUE........................ 8

ADVICE FOR TROUBLED TIMES 9

A LETTER FROM GRANDMAMA........................... 10

ALONE..11

ART APPRECIATION 12

AT THE PHILHARMONIC.................................. 13

BAGELS AND ROMANCE 14

BUTTERFLY IN THE CITY 15

CHILDHOOD FANTASY..................................... 16

COMPUTER BLUES 17

CRAZY QUILT 18

DREAMS 19

ENCHANTED APRIL....................................... 20

EVERY SWING SHOULD HAVE A TREE 21

FAIRY TALES WILL GET ME THROUGH THE WINTER 22

FAST SHOES.. 23

FOOLISH THINGS 24

GOING TO THE DOGS...................................... 25

HOW TO IMPRESS A VOLUNTEER: A DIALOG................. 26

IDENTITY CRISIS 28

I DON'T WANT TO MOVE................................... 29

I LOVE MYSTERIES 30

INSPIRATION 31

IRISH DREAMSCAPE....................................... 32

IT'S A PUZZLEMENT 33

LOVE LETTER 34

LOVERS OF PARIS 35

MEMORIES OF MARJORIE PRIME 36

MONEY DIDN'T MATTER................................... 37

MY ENORMOUS LIE.. 38

MY NEW RING... 40

MY PEOPLE 41

NEW YORK, NEW YORK 42

OUTDOOR SEATING ON FIRST AVENUE.................... 43

PAPER AIRPLANES. 44
PATIENCE AND POETRY. 45
PLACES I HAVE LIVED 46
REHEARSAL. 48
RUDEST CITY. 49
"R.U.R." 50
SENIOR BLUES 51
SHAKESPEARE'S ADVICE TO THE LOVELORN 52
SOUTHERN DISCOMFORT. 53
STATE FAIR 54
STORY FOR MOTHERS 55
STUDIES IN SCARLET. 56
SUNLIGHT AND SHADOW. 57
SUPERWOMAN 58
THE BOSTON SYMPHONY GETS DRESSED UP. 59
THE GREEKS HAVE A WORD FOR IT 60
THE LAST 10 YEARS. 61
THE PEOPLE I ENVY 62
THE PLAY'S THE THING. 63
THE UNSEEING EYE 64
THEATER TALK. 65
THEATRICAL SARAH. 66
TWO PROPOSALS 67
UP WITH ROMANCE 68
WAIT FOR SPRING. 69
WALKING COMPANIONS 70
WATERFALL. 71
WE GOT AWAY FROM IT ALL 72
WHEN I HEARD THE LEARNED ASTRONOMER 74
WHEN NANCY GOES TO SCHOOL 75
WHERE'S ANNABEL?. 76
WHY CARRY A CANE? 77
WILL THEY REMEMBER?. 78
WINTER WEATHER. 79
WORK (HELP WANTED). 80

A BEAUTIFUL DAY ON FIRST AVENUE

I watched the world go by on First Avenue,
Not just mothers and fathers pushing prams,
But skaters, scooters, runners,
A juggler magically moving a ball in the air,
A couple carrying home sections
Of a table they just bought,
He with the legs, she with the tabletop.
And crossing First Avenue, on a 90-degree day
All of the city in sweltering heat,
A tall, handsome man, naked to the waist,
Wearing only a pair of khaki shorts
On his beautiful brown body.
We greeted each other. Strangers no more.
I wished him "Good Morning!"
 "Hi Mama" he answered,
And gave me a thumbs up.
I said, "Beautiful Day!" and it **was**
A beautiful day on First Avenue.

ADVICE FOR TROUBLED TIMES

In this time of bleak recession,
How to fight against depression?
You'll have no bank account Hereafter;
The only thing to save is laughter.
The lack of stocks or bonds or money
Seems minor when your friends are funny.
Can't fund your yearly trip to Crete?
Stretch your legs on a New York street.
Get some inexpensive thrills
In Riverdale or Forest Hills.
When you read The New York Times,
And you weep at all the crimes,
Take a page from Scarlett's book,
Though you feel you are forsook,
Don't be killed with pain and sorrow —
Smile and shelve it 'til tomorrow.

A LETTER FROM GRANDMAMA

My great-grandson, Rowan, four years old,
Lives in Missouri. I see him twice a year,
Envying the grandparents whose little ones
Live downstairs, down the block, or in Connecticut.
I want him to connect with me,
And always to remember me,
But he has such excitement in his life:
A nanny, a new brother, books and puzzles,
And, of course, his mom and dad.
I'm not skillful with technology like Skype
Or FaceTime or text messaging,
So I decided instead to send him a letter —
A regular letter via the post office,
Also called "snail mail" by users of technology.
I enclosed a photo of myself, and a letter to him
Signed, "Love, Grandmama," since that's what he calls me.
I said I wanted him to remember me
And asked him to send me a photo of himself
In the stamped, addressed envelope enclosed.
Here's what I heard from his grandmother:
"Rowan was so thrilled to get your letter.
He was breathless as he told me the story.
He said his dad took it out of the mailbox
And it had Rowan's name on the envelope!
And Grandmama's picture was in it,
With a letter written just for him.
Rowan said he would send Grandmama his photo,
And HER dad would take it out of her mailbox,
And she would be so excited to see a letter from him."

In this ephemeral world
Where images disappear with a click,
MY heart yearns for permanence.
There is a power in words and pictures
That I can hold in my hand and keep
In a special place to look at again and again.

ALONE

I am alone, without company, all by myself,
Single, separate, solitary.
If I am lonely, who cares?
In America, nobody cares.
But in England, they have appointed
A Minister of Loneliness.

(In January, 2018, the UK appointed Tracey Crouch the Minister of Loneliness.)

ART APPRECIATION

On a trip to the Barnes Collection,
I gaze at curvaceous Renoirs.

When I visit the Met Museum,
I admire the Sargent portraits.

On a tour with friends to MOMA,
Picasso's sculptures amaze.

Long lines at the Neue Galerie
To enjoy Klimt's "Woman in Gold."

On the bus trip returning home
Those paintings fit in my purse.

Magnets keep all those favorites
Safe on my refrigerator door.

AT THE PHILHARMONIC

Seated directly in front of me — a teenaged couple.
From the backs of their heads, I observe that the boy is tall,
With jet black hair hanging neatly to his shoulders.
The girl, with a blondish chignon, several strands undone,
Shoulders bare in the air-conditioned hall.
The first movement of the symphony begins.
She lays her head upon his shoulder,
Nestling against his neck.
He sits upright, looking straight ahead,
Not resting his head against hers, not turning to smile,
Until she sits again straight in her seat.
A dozen times, through all four movements,
This sad pas de deux is repeated,
Her head on his shoulder, his body not responding.
When the music ends, he shows what flames his passion:
Applauding loudly, shouting "Bravo, Bravo!"
Her passion is for him. His, for the music.
What will become of this romance?
Can love blossom in such circumstance?
Perhaps.
Perhaps not.

BAGELS AND ROMANCE

Bagelworks on First Avenue
Sells a variety of bagels
To please anyone's taste.
I'm waiting for my order to be filled.

A woman behind me is talking
On a cellphone to her boyfriend.
"I'm at Bagelworks right now.
What kind of bagel do you want:
Sesame, whole wheat, pumpernickel
Sourdough, poppyseed, everything?
What? A plain bagel?" She is incredulous
And complains to the nearest stranger,
"I thought he was unique, unconventional,
And he orders a plain bagel. I may
Have to rethink this relationship."

"That man is in deep trouble," I say to myself
As I pay for my bagel order.
With an eye on my own relationships,
I take home sesame, sourdough, everything.

BUTTERFLY IN THE CITY

A teenager crosses East 61st Street
With a white butterfly
Circling around his head.

He opens his hand
Palm up, not to catch it
But to give the creature
A large landing field.

A white-haired lady
Crossing alongside him
Notices the butterfly
And smiles at a memory,
"Yesterday, one landed on my shoulder
 And stayed there for an hour."

They both smile in shared wonder
At the city's surprises.

CHILDHOOD FANTASY

Floating out of the Brooklyn Public Library,
A rainbow of fairy tales in my backpack,
A book opened in front of me, I drift
Down East 13th Street.

Tangled forests grow on the Brooklyn streets
Hiding castles where sleeping maidens lie.
As I cross Avenue O, trumpets sound,
"Long live the queen!"

Ogres pursue me up the stairs
Until with a golden key, I unlock the door
And find a haven on the couch
Where I can read happily ever after.

COMPUTER BLUES

After visiting twins who grow cuter and cuter,
I come home to the messages on my computer.
Looking for news, returning from travel,
I'm panning for gold, and just finding gravel:
Promotions, investments, increasing your wealth,
Exercise programs for physical health,
Opera, theater, concerts, and dance
I delete at random, with hardly a glance.
Disappointed with emails, I continue deleting.
What's this one? "Dear Grandma," I then keep on reading.
No increase of riches, but it can be told
With this email message, I now have struck gold.

CRAZY QUILT

Start with plush velvet, smooth satin, soft cotton shapes.
Maneuver them to find patterns:
Dark and light, plain and print.
Move and change
Until it looks right.
Embellish with ribbon and braid.
Embroider with feather stitches and French knots.
With sparkling threads, dream up stars.
Try new ones, rip them out, stitch again.
Learn from books, friends, teachers,
But in the end
Creating a crazy quilt
Is up to you
Alone.

DREAMS

In the dressing room
I put my arms through the sleeves
Of the apple-green jacket,
Feel the soft wool glide
Over my upper body
Like waves on a bay beach,
Gently caressing me.
I am Cinderella being dressed
In a gown of pure moonlight
By her fairy godmother.

All my dreams are woven
Into that designer jacket —
Dreams of travel around the world,
Owning a painting by Mary Cassatt,
Seeing Broadway shows
From the third row orchestra.

But even at half price,
It is too much to pay
For an apple-green dream,
So I coldly remove the jacket
And hang it on its hanger.
But I might look again
In a few more weeks.

Or I might take a trip around the world.

ENCHANTED APRIL

On a city street lined with pear trees,
An April breeze ruffles the branches.
Countless pear blossoms fall quietly,
Like snowflakes.

As I stare in wonder,
West 25th Street becomes a fairyland.
Do I alone sense the magic?
No...

A slender young Asian girl
Rises in the air to catch a blossom,
And having her prize in hand,
Turns to smile at me.

EVERY SWING SHOULD HAVE A TREE

Every swing should have a tree
Like this giant pine that's holding me.
Head back, my hair can reach the ground.
The creaking rope's the only sound,
And I'm so far from city swings
Held up by bars with iron rings.
Like chains to hold, it seems to me
That every swing should have a tree.

FAIRY TALES WILL GET ME THROUGH THE WINTER

This winter will not last forever.
The warm spring days to come will bring me gifts,
Like food to grandma from Red Riding Hood,
But with no wolf to frighten me.

This winter will not bring me to starvation.
I'll eat my porridge from the largest bowl.
I'll doze in my cozy bed through dark nights,
Waiting for the kiss of summer sunlight.

I will get through this frozen winter,
While crooked branches, dripping with icicles,
Scrape the window like long fingers of the witch
Poking Hansel and Gretel's soft young flesh.

No fairy tale — winter will disappear.
Spring will find me rejoicing in bright sunshine.
My heart will overflow with love while singing
Praises to this winter's *happy ending.*

FAST SHOES

Walking to the bank, using my cane,
I hurried to get there before closing time.

A father and daughter
Walked behind me, then passed me.
Laughing, he said, "I just told my daughter,
'That lady with the cane
Walks faster than me!'"
We all laughed, and he questioned,
"Were you ever a runner?"
"No, but I always walked fast," I replied.
"So now I still do, even with a cane."
We all laughed again.

And I remembered the day
When I walked with my husband
A long time ago,
And a fellow New Yorker
Pointed down at my feet,
And said to my husband,
"She has fast shoes!"
So I guess I still do.

FOOLISH THINGS
(for Arthur)

Self-published books where you were sole creator,
Your favorite joke about a Jewish waiter.

The reprint bought in an Old Lyme museum
City landmarks — how we love to see 'em.

A ramekin of luscious creme brûlée
A five-flight climb to see a classic play.

A photograph of foggy Mirror Lake
Classic films that kept us wide awake.

Foolish things — but absolutely true —
And everything reminds me of you.

GOING TO THE DOGS
Copper, Jack, Silas, Bentley, Garbo, Gina, Missy (and Mili)

On my trip to the Midwest,
Seeing family was the best.
But at each household — no regrets,
They introduced me to their pets.
This is a kind of monolog
Of how I got to know each dog.
Let me put this in the hopper;
I first meet Jack and lovely Copper.
They sleep and eat and hear us talk,
And twice a day we take a walk.
Then we visit Brad and Kate
With two more pets we think are great.
Great-grandkids there can all beguile us
As do their dogs, Bentley and Silas.
One is black and one is white
One is fierce, one a delight.
Then dinner with our friend named Jan;
We loved her shrimp dish in a pan.
Like the others, even more so,
We loved her dog whose name is Garbo.
Despite her name, she did not moan,
Or say, "I want to be alone."
From there we drove to Steve and Amy.
I love their dog and you can't blame me.
I'm sure you never could have seen a
Pet as nice as their dog Gina.
Then on to Nick and Emily
And kids, all very dear to me,
Whose dog, alert to any dangers,
Is not so comfortable with strangers.
The children love her; she's no sissy
They hug their big black dog named Missy.
(In closing you may think I'm silly
For adding Nancy's cat named Mili.)
So here is where I end my blogs
Of going to the cats and dogs.

HOW TO IMPRESS A VOLUNTEER: A DIALOG

Two kind young men —
A lawyer, a realtor
Donating their time
To talk with old people.
Eating together
In the community room
Of a senior residence.
I am the senior.

Lawyer:
"Where were you born?"

Senior
"Brooklyn."

Lawyer
"I live in Brooklyn now."

Senior
"It was very different then."

Lawyer
"What was different?"

Senior
"There were trolley cars
On Coney Island Avenue."

Lawyer
"When was that?
In the 50s?"

Senior
"No! In the 30s and 40s!"

Realtor
"And how do you pass
the time now?"

Senior
"Teaching and learning
at a program
affiliated with CUNY."

Realtor
"You teach at CUNY?"

Senior
"Yes. In a program
for retired people."

Realtor
"What do you teach?"

Senior
"Contemporary Poetry."

Realtor
"I don't know any
contemporary poetry.
And wouldn't know
where to find it."

Senior
"You might like Billy Collins.
He's really accessible.
You could look him up online."

Lawyer
"YOU'RE telling HIM to look online!"

Shock and Awe

IDENTITY CRISIS

I have one grandson;
He's like no other.
It's quite normal
For him to be formal.
He prefers to call me *grandmother*.

Twins Jake and Toby like to ride
Up and down on a seesaw.
Being different is a treat,
Both are smart and very sweet.
And they call me *great-grandma*.

With Ro, Max, and Josie
Wow! And Hurrah!
See me smile happily
When they call me *grandmama*.

Of theatrical Sarah,
(She's one of my lambs)
What joy she brings
When she dances and sings.
She lovingly calls me *grams*.

I like what they call me...
I know who I am.
So happy to be:
Their
grandmother
great-grandma
grandmama
AND grams.

I DON'T WANT TO MOVE

I don't want to move.
I've lived in Manhattan, Brooklyn, and Queens,
Nassau and Suffolk counties,
St. Louis, Missouri, and Memphis, Tennessee,
And I don't want to move.

I don't want to move.
Grew up in a three-room walkup,
Rattled around in a seven-room ranch,
Felt cozy in a five-room colonial,
Rented a split-level monster,
Enjoyed a doorman-guarded condo,
And I don't want to move.

I don't want to move.
I've had homes with attics and basements,
Garages and outdoor decks,
A home office with a bay window,
A sunroom overlooking a garden,
And I don't want to move.

Oh, well. There's the van.
Careful with that lamp!
It belonged to my mother...

I LOVE MYSTERIES

Though biographies and histories
Are books on which I binge,
My favorite tomes are mysteries,
Though violence makes me cringe.

When the detective looks for facts
Behind a grisly killing,
Done with a knife or with an axe,
With actions that are chilling,

Murder makes me feel alive,
I'm so ashamed to mention.
All my senses seem to thrive;
I'm in a new dimension.

Best of all, the great appeal
That I cannot resist:
Secrets often are revealed
In a most surprising twist!

The resolution is so clear
No hiding or pretending,
And all protagonists will hear
The final happy ending.

These mysteries inform my life
And teach me at this age,
When I myself encounter strife,
To smile and turn the page.

INSPIRATION
(for my mother)

On the balcony of a cruise ship, I saw
A vision, rising gracefully out of the fog:
Lady Liberty blessing New York Harbor,
A shadowy grey, with her lamp shining brightly.
Is that how she looked a hundred years ago
When a little Russian girl, hugging the smokestack
Of a different ship, gazed at her?
"An inspiration to us all,"
I used to say. Not speaking of the statue,
But of that little Russian girl who lit my way.

IRISH DREAMSCAPE

In a dream landscape in Ireland,
On a cobblestone walkway by a river,
Time moved in slow motion.
I leaned my cane against a metal fence
While taking a photo of an old stone church,
When my cane, looking for adventure,
Flew above the river, slowly falling,
Gracefully into the water below.

The memory of that cane floating through the air
Will be with me always.

I'm hoping that
As it drifted down the river, it landed
Near a cottage with a thatched roof
Inhabited by a woman of advanced age
Who needed some help with her walking,
And thinking it was the work of elves or fairies,
Used my cane happily ever after.

IT'S A PUZZLEMENT

With sharpened pencil in my room,
I meet my family group on Zoom.

Each week I join this grand event:
A crossword that's a puzzlement.

I love to solve a Shakespeare clue
Like, "eye source in a witch's brew."

The hint might be a funny one:
A far-fetched joke, a rhyme, a pun.

I want to give a word of thanks
For clues where you must fill in blanks.

But I'm not filled with great elation
When I must know a whole quotation!

Don't get upset. That's just absurd!
You must express not one Cross Word!

LOVE LETTER

Opening the title page
Of a book he had given me
Years ago for my birthday,
Handwritten words I didn't remember.

We had said our final goodbyes
So long ago, I could only assume
That a love letter, newly written
Had traveled through time to me.

"I knew you would be
Even more wonderful at 60
Than you were when you were 20.
Love, Love, Love, Forever."

So we are still connected
Through words and memories…

This much I have learned —
Nothing is final, even goodbye.

LOVERS OF PARIS

On the 37 bridges crossing the Seine
Parisian men and women pledge their love:
They attach a padlock to the side of the bridge,
Lock it and toss the key into the dark water.
Will he be faithful because the key
Is sleeping at the bottom of the Seine?
Will she turn from temptation because her promise
Is locked on a bridge near the indifferent waters?

*****

Lovers of Paris — stay true to each other,
Though life flows by like currents in the river.
May joy outlast the strongest metal clasp,
And love be locked in your hearts forever.

MEMORIES OF *MARJORIE PRIME*

Some years ago
I fell in love with a play
Called *Marjorie Prime*
About artificial intelligence.

Because of the way
The years have piled up,
Marjorie has a sense of loss
So she shares her memories
With a hologram
Who looks exactly like
Her husband when young.
He remembers all,
Helping her to become more human.

To hold onto my memories,
Instead of a hologram,
I talk to my daughters
Who remind me of the past,
What they said,
What I did,
How we felt when it happened.

As a daughter myself,
I listened to stories
Of my mother's childhood
In the Ukraine.
I passed her tales onward
To children and grandchildren
So they will remember her.

In shared memories, we live forever.

MONEY DIDN'T MATTER

You never showed distress,
When I purchased a new dress
Or coat or hat.
Money didn't matter.
You never asked what I paid.
I would parade
In front of you in my new clothes
And you would never impose
Your opinions on my taste
Or suggest I bought in haste.
I loved that about you
Although I admit, it's also true
That when we shopped
For you, I never stopped
You from buying suits
At Brooks Brothers.
You were absolutely
Great at choosing ties
That went well with your blue eyes.
People may think it odd
Because money was not our god.
Buying things was pleasurable we found,
But it was love that made the world go round.

MY ENORMOUS LIE

Southwest Airlines
Has no reserved seats.
As you enter the plane,
You decide where you'll sit.
I wanted a seat
Near the front on the aisle,
But they were all gone.
I decided instead
On a seat in the middle.
I did NOT plan to sit
At the emergency exit,
But I plopped myself down,
And fastened my seat belt.
I learned there were rules.

They asked the young woman
In the seat on the aisle
"Are you over 15?"
(I wasn't asked.)
But along came another,
Stared sharply at me,
"Are you ready and able
In case of emergency
To open the door,
Help folks to escape,
And move out the baggage?"
No answer at first.
I said, "If you doubt,
You can find a new seat,
And I will move there."
She quickly replied.
"It's all up to you,
I can't make you move.
Can you do the job?"

I thought of my arm
Needing physical therapy.
I thought of my balance
That is not of the best.
It was then that I told
My enormous lie,
"I think I can do it."

And she walked away.
I stared at the door
With the handle to pull,
Relieved that a fellow
So young and so strong
Sat by the window.

I tried to compose
Some comforting thoughts:
Some alien beings
Might hijack the plane
And take us to galaxies
Far, far away.
Then I won't have to open
The emergency door
And I won't have to save
The people and luggage.

We safely hit ground,
And then with a sigh,
I happily found
We all had survived.
I had gladly outlived
My enormous lie.

MY NEW RING

Impressionist painting
Surrounded by silver;
Azure sky at twilight
With sparkling pink stars.

This ring was a gift
I bought for myself
To honor my wedding
Sixty-four years ago.

How do I know
What he would have chosen?
He could read my mind
And he knew I loved
Impressionist paintings.

MY PEOPLE

Residing at a senior facility
I live with ease and with tranquility,
Enjoying lovely meals each day
With friendly diners, Anne and Ray,
And other folks who may attend.
It's easy, there, to be a friend.

I wonder why, all being equal,
Some folks may call these friends, "my people."
It's true that it does seem a pity
They never lived in New York City,
And I don't come from Illinois
Or Alabama, though it's a joy
To hear about their childhood days...
And we agree in many ways.

In trying not to be confused,
I find that "peeps" is often used.
And now it often haunts my sleep
That "people" is renamed as "peeps."
And here is where my question ends:
As long as peeps are my good friends,
It seems that *peeps* won't go away...
I'm glad *my peeps* are here to stay.

NEW YORK, NEW YORK

To some folks who grew up on farms
New York City rings alarms.
"Can you get through the day unhurt?
Are the subways filled with dirt?
I hear the park is even worse!
At night, hold tightly to your purse!"

No, no, as I have oft discussed,
This bleak description is unjust.
It's understood that bad or good
Folks live in every neighborhood.

I can spend my New York days
Attending great museums and plays.
What fun to ride upon a landmark:
The carousel in Central Park.
Like reading? Well, with fearsome looks,
Two lions guard its many books.
There is so very much to see,
When you explore its history.

As I am a New York defender,
I smile as I enjoy its splendor!

OUTDOOR SEATING ON FIRST AVENUE

On First Avenue and 61st Street
In front of Bed Bath & Beyond,
There are comfortable metal seats —
A city dweller's front porch,
A window on city life.

Looking across First Avenue,
I can see a red brick building,
Haunting and symmetrical,
Like a painting by Hopper,
With storefronts beneath.

On the sidewalk,
People with packages,
Couples, dog walkers,
Nannies pushing baby carriages.
In the street, police cars, trucks,
Taxis, stopping for a fare.
Overhead, the tramway travels
On its voyage to Roosevelt Island.
I too am on a voyage,
Living the magic of city life.
And enjoying the ride.

PAPER AIRPLANES

The floor under the tree is covered with toys:
Robots, Legos, puzzles, and games,
Coloring books, sticker books, storybooks,
Crayons, paints, and brushes.
So why are the children
Ignoring them all?
Watching their Grandpa
Take a large sheet of paper
And turn it and fold it
And hold it in a way
That when he thrusts it in air,
It flies across the room
To the star on top of the tree,
Or over the ceiling fan,
Getting stuck on the blades.
The children, the pilots,
Have to turn on the switch
So the fan will dislodge
Its resident airplane.
It is so much fun,
The grownups fly too,
Restoring their memories
Of a long-ago life.

Grandchildren's memories
Are now newly born
On the day that they gladly
Neglected their toys
To explore outer space
With Grandpa's creative,
Mystical, remarkable, life-affirming
Paper airplanes!

PATIENCE AND POETRY

I've always been adept
At taking out the knots
That appear mysteriously
In shoelaces, yarn, and string.
It's truly satisfying
To unravel the strands
Using my hands and fingers
And restore to its proper state
That which is in chaos.

"It shows that you have patience,"
My mother used to say.
That may be so.
But what makes it intriguing
Are the twists and connections,
Like a riddle you need to puzzle out.

Poetry is like that too,
Except instead of hands and fingers,
You use imagination
To unravel the meaning.
And a little patience helps too.

PLACES I HAVE LIVED

Brooklyn
My sister and I did not talk gloom and doom,
Though we slept on a couch in the living room.
A few years later, almost grown
We were given a bedroom all our own.

Queens
With my new husband, I had the means
To move to a building in Bayside, Queens.

Nassau County
Family growing, we needed space
Glen Cove was a nice suburban place.

With the loss of a job we looked around,
Found a cozy home in Levittown.

St. Louis
A new job offer in the Midwest
St. Louis County seemed the best.
A place of comfort and of charm
We bought a house in Oak Tree Farm.

Memphis
Daughters to college to get a degree
Husband transferred to Tennessee.

Nassau County (reprise)
New York was calling; we formed a committee
To look for a home in Garden City.

Suffolk County
Living in Southold, life was a peach
We started a business and sat on the beach.

New York City
It was time for Manhattan; we were retired,
Time to enjoy the things we desired.
So I live on the East Side after trying the West,
And I think I have found the place I like best.
So I don't plan to move, whatever the price
'Til they find me a penthouse in Paradise.

Westbury Senior Living — 2023
Nearer to family, in the Midwest.
I finally discovered what suits me the best.
There's no discussion; there's no debate.
Paradise will have to wait!

REHEARSAL

In my meditation session
Our teacher revealed
That monks try to simulate dying
To understand how it would feel
To endure this ultimate experience.
I have tried to replicate their endeavors
In my leather chair in a deep sleep.
I failed. I could not pretend to die
Or even imagine heaven.

But when I was in a crowded cafe
Attached to an off-Broadway theater
With music screaming in my ears
And people squeezed like lemons,
Talking at the top of their lungs
It was like a hint of hell.
Then doors opened for me
And the usher took my ticket.
Finally, I was able to enter
The heavenly peace of the theater.

RUDEST CITY
(TRAVEL + LEISURE Poll: "New York Voted Rudest City
in the U.S.A.")

When you think of rudeness, don't think of us —
I am given a seat on the subway or bus.
Riding calmly through traffic, I'm satisfied
When folks thank the driver for their ride.

In the subway, a MetroCard machine
Made me feel grim and a little green,
But I had to buy one for a guest.
A young man saw my urgent request.
As a New York City samaritan,
He showed me the steps so that now *I can.*

On a bus, met a friend and with a smile,
I was talking to her across the aisle,
A passenger stood to change seats with me,
So my friend and I could talk easily.

Home from a show, Playbill on my knee
Fellow riders will ask, "What did you see?"
"Oh, yes, I saw that performance, too.
What would you give it in your review?"

On a city bus, in the driver's seat,
The man helped me find a particular street.
He joked, like a caring chaperone,
"Be sure to call me when you get home!"

It's not a secret! You can shout it.
Rudest city? Fuggetaboutit!

"R.U.R."

(Title of a play, subtitled, "Rossum's Universal Robots" by
Karel Capek, written in 1920, in which the word "robot" was
introduced.)

My great-grandson, Rowan
Got a robot for Christmas.
It has a name: Cosmo.
It has a personality —
Not nerdy, sci-fi and high-tech,
But ego-driven, self-absorbed,
Sensitive, cranky, and appealing.
Rowan plays games with it.
It is adorable, funny, and so human.
When Cosmo wins, it raises its "arms"
In the air and shouts something like "Yay!"
When it loses, it turns away,
Mutters, complains, and sulks.
R.U.R., Rowan's Ultimate Robot —
Is this what the world needs now?

When I am lonely and tired of books,
And television has lost its charm,
Seeking a human connection,
I may buy Cosmo for myself.
I am almost convinced
That this could be the beginning
Of a beautiful friendship.

SENIOR BLUES

Promenading on a summer's day
Sunny and breezy, I'm taking an airing.
Stopped by a lady, well-dressed and gray
Who says, "I like what you are wearing.
From where I stand, I can easily see
That you are a senior just like me."
I smile and am happy to agree...
On the city sidewalk, under a tree,
She continues the conversation,
"Now I'm on YouTube where you can see
That I could be called a singing sensation.
Watch when you have a moment free.
I wrote the music and words to this song
And I'll sing it for you right this minute
If you have the time, it won't take long,
And I'll put my best performance in it."
I do not move; I do not stir.
Standing in my brand new shoes,
I hear the poet and composer
Sing a song called "Senior Blues."

There are people who believe that life
In Gotham City is never sweet,
Just sad and gritty and filled with strife.
But oh, the magic you might meet
On any New York City street!

SHAKESPEARE'S ADVICE TO THE LOVELORN
("Brush up your Shakespeare. Start quoting him now."
From Kiss Me Kate)

Q. Can't stop crying, can't stop sighing. Will this go on forever?
A. "Sigh no more ladies, sigh no more. Men were deceivers ever."
(Much Ado About Nothing)

Q. Shall I shout my feelings to heaven above?
A. "Speak low, if you speak love."
(Much Ado About Nothing)

Q. Should I say I adore him in a passionate letter?
A. "Love sought is good, but given unsought is better."
(Twelfth Night)

Q. Lasting peace between lovers? Is that an untruth?
A. "The course of true love never did run smooth."
(A Midsummer Night's Dream)

Q. My love is away. Will he be true to me?
A. "Lord, what fools these mortals be!"
(A Midsummer Night's Dream)

SOUTHERN DISCOMFORT

Brought up in New York City,
But living in the South in the 60s,
I shocked the inhabitants
By sitting down
At a drugstore counter
And ordering
A "black and white" ice cream soda.

STATE FAIR

On a winter's night in 2011,
I watched a movie made in 1945,
In Technicolor™ bright as a lollipop.

Jeanne Crain sat in the window
Of her Iowa farmhouse
In the heat of a summer's day
And sang, "It Might As Well Be Spring."

I was 14 years old in 1945,
Looking out on clotheslines
From the window of my Brooklyn apartment,
Feeling "restless as a willow in a windstorm."

Seventy-five years later, I can remember how it felt
To be 14 and looking for love.
The miracle was that I found it,
and it will always be with me.

That's even better than a Hollywood ending.

STORY FOR MOTHERS

When my daughters were small,
One of their favorite stories
Was about a turtle
Whose mother would caution him
About the dangers in the world.

"Don't touch that stove,"
His mother would say,
"It's hot! and could burn you."
Then he would touch it
And say, "OOh, it's hot!"

Or, "That water is too cold,"
His mother would say,
"Stay out of it. You'll freeze."
He would go anyway
And say, "OOh, it's cold!"

My daughters used that turtle
As their role model.
They dipped their fingers and toes
into marriages and careers
Their mother warned them against.

They made their own way
Into meaningful lives,
Which only goes to prove
That in our family,
Turtle knows best.

STUDIES IN SCARLET

1. "A Study in Scarlet" by Sir Arthur Conan Doyle
The very first of many tomes
About detective Sherlock Holmes —
When it was published as a book,
Few readers deigned to take a look.
Today, this book, preserved with care
Could make the owner a millionaire.

2. "The Scarlet Pimpernel" by Baroness Emmuska Orczy
We seek it here; we seek it there,
We seek adventure anywhere.
A tale of one who's good and wise,
A superhero in disguise,
Pretends to be a wimp, a coward
(Played in the film by Leslie Howard).
The book reveals the violent error,
Ending, at last, The Reign of Terror.

3. "The Scarlet Letter" by Nathaniel Hawthorne
Hester Prynne, where have you been,
With your husband far away?
A baby girl, whose name is Pearl
And your scarlet letter "A"
Show you have been engaged in sin,
And there will be hell to pay.

4. "The Ballad of Reading Gaol" by Oscar Wilde
"He did not wear his scarlet coat..."
I know the reason why.
His scarlet coat would simply clash
With his dazzling purple tie.

SUNLIGHT AND SHADOW

Sitting outdoors on First Avenue
Basking in the bright sunlight —
Suddenly a shadow overhead
Darkens my world.

No planes flying above me
No rain clouds in the sky
But the tramway to Roosevelt Island
Has cast a shadow over me.

I shiver. Everything might change
In the space of a second...
A dark moment has come and gone
And I am back in the brilliant sunlight.

SUPERWOMAN

Long black hair billowing behind her,
A floor-length purple cloak on her back,
Floating above her high-heeled shoes —
She runs past me on East 61st Street.

Is she rushing to catch the Third Avenue bus?
Or late for the W train to wake up Wall Street?
A glance at her face will give me a clue.
I turn the corner. She is gone.

No bus has arrived. Subway stairs — empty.
Is she flying above the traffic on Third Avenue,
Purple cloak lifting her aloft? Look! Up in the sky!
A purple light shines in the misty morning.

THE BOSTON SYMPHONY GETS DRESSED UP

Rehearsal. Boston Symphony.
The audience: a handful of music lovers
At Tanglewood in the Berkshires,
In the Koussevitzky Music Shed.
Cellphones off! No applause please.

Conductor in a navy polo shirt,
Two cellists sport baseball caps,
Clarinetist wears plaid,
Second violinist in a yellow skirt,
Trumpet player in jeans.

Rehearsing the symphony,
The conductor sings the notes
Directing and inspiring the orchestra.
Melodious themes are replayed
By musicians in casual clothes.

The day of the concert
The music shed bursting with people.
Musicians enter the stage
Wearing white jackets, black trousers
And black bowties on the men.
No baseball caps, no yellow skirt.

The conductor enters to wild applause
Raises his baton and the music starts —
A gift for the audience
Beautifully wrapped in white and black.

THE GREEKS HAVE A WORD FOR IT

Unknown neighborhood
Way on the Westside.
Restaurant recommended
By a forgetful friend
Who gave the wrong address.

Should I keep looking
On both sides of the street?
For The Greek Kitchen
When the clock keeps ticking?
Or ask somebody?

Many people strolling
Along 10th Avenue.
I should choose one person
Who may know the neighborhood.
A woman's walking toward me.

"Have you ever heard of
The Greek Kitchen restaurant
Located nearby?" I asked.
"Sure! I'm having lunch there.
Follow me," she offered.

How did I decide
To ask the one woman
Walking on 10th Avenue
Who would definitely know?
Perhaps the Greeks have a word for it.

(It's "telepathy.")

THE LAST 10 YEARS

Standing in an endless line,
I talked to a man
Who told me
In a confident voice
That he planned to travel
The last 10 years of his life.

My mind did somersaults.
"How will you know
When the last 10 years will be?
You may be dead tomorrow!"

He opened his eyes wide.
"I've told that to so many people,
And they never argued with me."

The line moved so slowly
I almost forgot
What would be waiting for us
When we got to the end.

THE PEOPLE I ENVY

The wives whose husbands are alive,
The folks who suffered and survived.
Hikers, skiers, climbers, walkers,
And all New Yorkers.

Poets who make their readers cry
Folks who easily say "goodbye."
People who feel that life is fun.
Anyone younger than 91.

THE PLAY'S THE THING

I'm so stuffed with emotion, I can hardly contain
The tingling excitement that inhabits my brain.
As I wait for the time when the lights start to dim
And the curtain goes up, I am filled to the brim
With wonder about the magic to come.
Will the scene be a mansion or a ghetto-like slum?
What stories? What Insights? What hopes and what fears?
Will I be inspired? Will it move me to tears?
Will the playwright be seen as another O'Neill?
Will the actors amaze with portrayals so real?

Or, despite my playgoer's intuition,
If the playwright has offered a poor submission,
Will I be leaving at intermission?

THE UNSEEING EYE

In a test
Of observation skills
My class was told
To watch a short film
And count
The number of times
A ball was thrown
From one player
To another.

I counted the throws.
But what did I NOT see?
"Did you see the gorilla?"
Our teacher asked.
Gorilla? What gorilla?
A gorilla had sidled into the film
And out again
Without my noticing.

So I ask myself
"What are you NOT seeing
As you walk the New York streets?
A purple tulip
Enshrouded in trash?
An indistinct angel
Waiting at the traffic light?
Or mysterious words
From a line in a poem
To awaken your unseeing eye?"

THEATER TALK

I'm confused and not quite certain
When the stagehands close the curtain,
If theater helps us thrive,
Or makes us sad to be alive.
I realize that it's very hard
To make a living as a bard
But why can't writers make us laugh?
Must they design an epitaph?
When I buy a play subscription,
My doctor gives me a prescription
To overcome my deep depression.
Why can't they teach an upbeat lesson,
Instead of trying to beguile
The audience and make them smile?
They write of illness, death, and war.
What did I purchase tickets for?
It is no use to keep pretending
To look for plays with happy endings.

THEATRICAL SARAH

Sarah is a singer
An actor
An artist
A hoop dancer.
(Don't call them "Hula Hoops™."
That's so last century.)
She decorates her hoops
With colored ribbons
And light-emitting diodes
And sometimes fire!
(I've only seen her dance with fire
On my computer. Not in person.
I'm glad about that.)
Her stage name is Surka Noelle.
(Surka was my mother's Russian name.)
I watch her twirl
Those enormous rings
Around her body
With perfect grace.

I'm so proud that Sarah
Is my granddaughter.

TWO PROPOSALS

For two days in February, the weather turned balmy
And I was involved in some daring adventures —
I received two proposals on two city buses.
I never imagined a bus was romantic.
It may be a case of early spring fever.

It began with a man on the crosstown bus.
"How are you doing? You look nice. Are you married?
"A widow," I said. "I'd like to marry you," said he.
I said, "Your proposal is my first one today."
"Today!" he laughed. And I laughed too.

The next was a chat on the First Avenue bus
With a man revealed as "a tourist from Queens."
He said, "You're so nice, I'd like to take you home."
I smiled and replied, "I have a home, thank you."
I suppose he returned to Queens by himself.

Maybe I should be a little more wary
But I've decided to look for adventure,
So I'm planning a bus trip on the next balmy day.

UP WITH ROMANCE

Riding on the DOWN escalator
In the subway at 59th and Lex,
I stared at a couple on the UP escalator,
Kissing as they moved through space,
He one step above her,
She reaching her lips up to his.
What awed me most as I held tightly
To the moving black banister
Was How do they keep their balance?
LOVE and YOUTH, I answered myself,
Stepping nimbly off the escalator steps,
Using, of course, my indispensable cane.

WAIT FOR SPRING

On a weary winter night
Memories are quick to spring,
Cat-like, to the waiting mind
And settle down to dream.

And while the winter wails outside,
With words to sigh, sad songs to sing.
My dreams and I beside the fire
Can stretch and sleep and wait for spring.

WALKING COMPANIONS

My daughter walks
With a friend each day.
I have no friends
Who love to take long walks.
So I walk alone in the city streets,
Watching the dog walkers expertly
Leading on leashes three or four canines,
Large, small, many different breeds:
Beagles, collies and spaniels,
Walking quietly, contentedly
On city streets with their dog walker.

Could there be a people walker
For folks like me without companions?
Couldn't we benefit from the friendship
Of three or four folks, large and small,
Many different ethnicities?
I'm sure we would walk quietly, contentedly,
Getting acquainted with each other,
Enjoying the rich friendships
That develop as we meander
Along the city streets.

WATERFALL

Traveling in the Canadian Rockies,
A falling ribbon of water beckoned to me.
I left the group and hiked right up to it.
A torrent of silver cascading earthward,
It laughed and danced its way down to the ground.
A living thing, it sprayed my face with mist.
Engulfed in mystery and beauty,
Connected to a force beyond my knowledge,
I had a fleeting glimpse of the eternal.

More than orange-gold sunsets,
More than majestic mountains,
The spirit of the waterfall had moved me.
I felt we shared a sacred moment.
Alone with my secret, I walked back on the path,
Mist on my face, mingling with my tears.

WE GOT AWAY FROM IT ALL

We took a journey to Old Lyme,
Saw Connecticut leaves in the fall,
With Regina and Farbers,
Sailed Baltimore harbor.
We got away from it all.

Had a candlelight breakfast in New Hope.
In Philly, toured Liberty's Hall,
Viewed Matisse and Courbet
And Renoir and Manet.
We got away from it all.

Toured Newport to look at "The Breakers."
Saw rooms where the rich had a ball.
Peggy put on mascara,
And wore her tiara.
We got away from it all.

We stayed at a farm called Sweet Water
Polo ponies ran free near their stalls.
The niece of Grace Kelly
Served us coffee and jelly.
We got away from it all.

We strolled through exhibits at Shelburne
And didn't mind walking at all.
On a porch by the lake,
They served high tea with cake.
We got away from it all.

We ate at some Williamsburg taverns,
And heard freedom's original call.
We saw William and Mary
(And of the stocks we were wary.)
We got away from it all.

We took a trip to Bar Harbor.
We shivered and wished for a shawl.
We ate lobster galore,
And we shopped every store.
We got away from it all.

Then we were off to the Berkshires,
For music, theatre, et al.
Our adventures seem tame,
Yet our joy will remain,
For we'd had such a ball
That we'd always recall
How we got away from it all.

WHEN I HEARD THE LEARNED ASTRONOMER
(Inspired by Walt Whitman's "When I Heard the Learned Astronomer")

When I heard the learned astronomer,
I listened in awe-inspired wonder.

When did the universe give birth
To the planets, such as Earth?

How many stars are in the sky?
We cannot count or even try.

Like Whitman, I could not contain
The facts that buzzed about my brain.

But looking up from Earth, our home,
The star-filled sky was like a poem.

WHEN NANCY GOES TO SCHOOL

When Nancy goes to school, she brings
Bags and bags and bags of things!
A lunchbox with a lid that zips
A tuna sandwich and potato chips,
A schoolbag with a buckle that snaps,
Textbooks, notebooks, and hand-drawn maps.
On days she plays in the Junior Band,
Don't forget clarinet and music stand.
Sneakers twice a week, for exercise.
Statues for art class, when the plaster dries.
And right after school, when the Girl Scouts meet,
She needs her uniform, so green and neat.

On Nancy's birthday, would she make a fuss
If we bought her, for a present, an octopus?
With those eight arms, he could carry everything,
While Nancy plans on the **extras** she could bring!

WHERE'S ANNABEL?

Where's Annabel? It's time for bed.
Her covers are down; her story's been read.
Is she off in the barn? Is she out in the stable?
Is she down in the dining room, under the table?
Is she up in the attic with boxes and things?
Is she climbing a tree? Is she high on the swings?
I don't seem to see her. I've looked all around.
But hush! Now I think I hear some kind of sound.
It comes from the basket where the kittens all sleep.
I'll just tiptoe over and take a small peep.
The mother and three little kittens makes four.
But I look near the basket, and there is one more.
Curled up like a kitten, and yet I can tell,
The one in pajamas is my Annabel!

WHY CARRY A CANE?

Perhaps it may seem foolish to explain
The many clever uses for a cane.
I do not find your ignorance appalling
If you believe it's just to keep from falling.
And traveling on the subway, it's so neat
That males and females offer you a seat.

What other things can canes be useful for?
For thrusting though an elevator door
Instead of holding open with your arm
So that your arm will never come to harm.

You're on a bus and waiting for your stop.
How can you pull the wire near the top?
Glance at the ceiling. Take a measured look.
Then use your cane just as you would a hook.
If you behave as I have just suggested,
You'll see the sign light up now: STOP REQUESTED.

Essential in all weathers is my cane.
It keeps me safe from snow and wind and rain,
Avoiding slippery stuff that I might step on —

On dark nights, I could use it as a weapon!

WILL THEY REMEMBER?
(A visit from my four-year-old great-grandsons)

Looking down from the plane window to count boats in the
river?
Peeking through a fence to see the excavators digging?
Gazing on the museum roof at a crane atop a skyscraper?
Eyeing gigantic dinosaurs with teeth like daggers?
Admiring graceful skaters at Rockefeller Center?
Will they remember the sounds of sirens on the city streets?
And their laughter as they rode the carousel in Central Park?

They will remember. Because my grown-up granddaughter,
Remembers, "When I was five-years-old
My family took me to "Phantom of the Opera."
I told my grandmother I wanted to be Christine.
She said, 'Of course you can my darling,'
So I studied music and dance, and that's my life now."

Yes. I think they will remember.

WINTER WEATHER

Snowstorms keep battering us;
The icy sidewalks dare me to plant my feet
On their slippery surface. Mounds of the white stuff
Keep me separated from the bus that will take me home.

Home, where it is warm, where I can heat a cup
Of dark cocoa topped with mini-marshmallows.
Walking home from the bus stop, icy pitfalls everywhere,
A woman offers me her arm — angel in a fur-lined hoodie.

WORK (HELP WANTED)

My mother left school at 13,
Wrapped her braids around her head,
And went to work for a milliner.
She didn't have working papers,
So when the inspector came,
They hid her in a storeroom.

At 18, she applied for a job
At Metropolitan Life Insurance Company.
"We don't hire Jewish girls," they told her,
But the manager said, "I'll give you a try,"
And they liked her work so well
They asked her to recommend a friend.
"I have a cousin who's a good worker,
But she's Jewish too," said my mother,
And that's how she broke down barriers
At the Brooklyn office of Met Life.

Milton Keynes UK
Ingram Content Group UK Ltd.
UKHW020848030624
443491UK00014B/359

9 798218 358167